Copyright © 1988 by Gerald Rose
All rights reserved.

Aladdin Books
Macmillan Publishing Company
866 Third Avenue, New York, NY 10022

Published simultaneously by Methuen
Children's Books, Ltd., London

Printed in Hong Kong
by Wing King Tong Co Ltd

10 9 8 7 6 5 4 3 2 1

ISBN 0-689-71197-2

Cataloging-in-Publication Data is available.

A FABLE BY AESOP
The Hare and the Tortoise

Retold and illustrated by Gerald Rose

Aladdin Books
Macmillan Publishing Company
New York

The tortoise said to the hare, "I will give you this juicy apple if you race me round that distant tree and get back to this same spot before me. And of course," added the tortoise, "if you lose the race, that crispy carrot you are nibbling will be mine."

The hare looked at the distant tree
and was in no doubt as to who was
the faster runner. He instantly agreed.

An umpire was chosen to start the race and to look after the juicy apple and crispy carrot.

Off they went.

The hare thought, "If I run this race as if a fox is after me it will be no fun." So he stopped and nibbled the grass

and acted the fool.

Then he waited for slowpoke.

As soon as slowpoke caught up with him he shot off again like a rocket.

He reached the tree in a flash
and lay down to rest.

When the hare finally woke up
the tortoise could not be seen.

The hare ran as if all the hounds in the land
were after him...

but he was too late. The tortoise came in first.

Sometimes it is better to be slow but sure.